Table of Contents

INTRODUCTION

To build a successful business, you need more than a good—or even great—idea. You have to be well organized, flexible, and creative, and develop a knack for paying close attention to the details while never losing sight of the big picture. You should also be prepared to make some personal sacrifices. Whatever type of business you have in mind, these nine basic tips, with links to additional advice, can help you get it started and keep it growing.

9 TIPS FOR GROWING A SUCCESSFUL BUSINESS

1. Get Organized

To achieve success as a business owner you first have to be well organized. That will help you complete tasks efficiently and stay on top of the many things that need to be done. A simple way to get and stay organized is to create a to-do list each day. As you complete each item, check it off your list. Remember, too, that some tasks are more important than others. Aim to tackle the high-priority ones first. There are many online resources that are available to help. They include tools like Slack, Asana, Zoom, and Microsoft Teams. That being said, a simple Excel spreadsheet will meet many of a small business's organizational requirements, especially in the early days.

2. Keep Detailed Records

No matter how busy they are, successful businesses take the time to keep careful accounting records. By doing so, they know where their business stands financially and can often get a better (and earlier) grasp of any potential challenges they might be facing. Investopedia periodically rates the best accounting software for small businesses. Many businesses today keep two sets of records: one physical and another in the cloud. That way, a business owner no longer has to worry about losing crucial data if something unfortunate happens, like a fire, computer virus, or other calamity.

3. Analyze Your Competition

To be successful, you can't afford to ignore your competitors. Instead, take the time to study and learn from them. Larger companies devote significant resources to obtaining this sort of competitive intelligence.

How you go about analyzing the competition can depend on the nature of your business. If you're a restaurant or store owner, you may simply be able to dine or shop at a competitor's place of business, ask customers what they like or don't like about it, and gain information that way. If you're in a field with more limited access to your competitors' inner workings, such as manufacturing, try to keep up with the news in relevant trade publications, speak with any customers you share in common, and obtain and scrutinize whatever financial information a competitor makes publicly available.

4. Understand the Risks and Rewards

Another key to being successful is taking calculated risks to help your business grow. Besides contemplating the potential rewards if you succeed, a good question to ask is: "What's the downside if this doesn't work out?" If you can answer that question, you'll know what the worst-case scenario is. If you could live with that scenario, and are prepared to take the necessary steps to manage the risk as much as possible, you might want to give it a go. Otherwise, this could be a good time to consider other opportunities. Understanding risks and rewards includes being smart about the timing of starting a business or launching a new product. For example, the severe economic dislocation during the COVID pandemic provided some businesses with new opportunities (say, manufacturing and selling protective gear) and others with difficult-to-overcome obstacles (such as running a restaurant with constraints on indoor dining).

5. Be Creative

Always be looking for ways to improve your business and make it stand out from the competition. Recognize that you don't know everything and be open to new ideas and different approaches. Keep an eye out for opportunities to expand your current business or develop related enterprises that will lead to additional revenues and provide the benefit of diversification. The history of Amazon provides a good example. The company started out as an online bookseller and grew into an e-commerce giant, selling just about everything. Today it has a growing brick-and-mortar presence, as well. Among its many subsidiaries are

Amazon Pharmacy, Amazon MGM Studios, Whole Foods Market, and Zappos.6. Stay Focused on Your Goals

The old saying "Rome wasn't built in a day" applies to building a business as well. Just because you open a business doesn't mean you're going to start making money immediately. It takes time to let people know who you are and what you have to offer, so stay focused on achieving your goals. Even many small business owners who ultimately achieve success won't see a profit for a few years and will have to rely on borrowed money (if they can get it) or their own savings to support the business until it can become profitable. Fortunately, there are a variety of ways to finance a business. That being said, if the business is not turning a profit after a reasonable period of time, it's worth looking into why that is and whether the business needs to go in another direction.

7. Provide Great Customer Service

Too many businesses forget the importance of providing great customer service. If you deliver better service for your customers, they'll be more inclined to come to you the next time they need something instead of going to your competition. High-quality service is one key to obtaining competitive advantage in the marketplace. Some businesses refer to this as a taking a consumer-centric or client-centric approach. In fact, in today's hyper-competitive business environment, service is often the major differentiating factor between successful and unsuccessful businesses. This is where the saying "undersell and overdeliver" comes in, and savvy business owners are wise to follow it.

8. Be Consistent

Consistency is a key component to success in business. You have to keep doing what is necessary to be successful, day in and day out. This will create long-term positive habits that will help you make money in the long run and create satisfied customers from day one. Customers value consistency, too.

9. Prepare to Make Some Sacrifices

Having your own business often requires putting in more time than if you were working for someone else. That can mean spending less time with family and friends than you wish you could. The adage that there are no weekends and no vacations for business owners can ring true for anyone who's committed to making their business work. Owning a business isn't for everyone. If, after an honest self-evaluation, you decide you aren't cut out for it, you'll save yourself a lot of grief, and probably a lot of money, by pursuing another career path.

What Is the Fastest Way for a Business to Grow?

Businesses will grow at their own rates, and many times this is out of the control of the business owner or workers. However, there are some aspects to running lean that may help a business grow quickly, such as focusing on a small product line, scaling up at a manageable pace, and providing some sort of obvious edge over your competitors.

How Do You Increase Sales?

Increasing sales can come from a few different places. You can raise ad expenditures where advertising has already proven effective, proactively solicit referrals from existing clients, build a direct-to-consumer email list, and others. You can also expand your product portfolio, but if the new additions underperform, that will negatively affect your bottom line.

What Makes a Startup Successful?

Business success is a difficult concept to quantify, but if it means generating returns for stakeholders, startups can be an excellent way to deliver returns. The best startups have a good product or service that is scalable. A well-run startup will understand the overall market and its particular place in it, be able to pivot quickly, and be ready to take advantage of opportunities when they present themselves.

Growing a successful business is hard work, and not everyone succeeds at it. According to 2022 data from the U.S. Bureau of Labor Statistics, about 20% of new businesses fail during their first year, 50% fail during the first five years, and 65% fail during the first 10 years. Only

25% of new businesses make it to 15 years or beyond. If you want to be among that 25%, paying attention to these nine tips is a good start, but certainly not exhaustive. To own and run a successful business you'll want to be in a state of constant learning and adapting.

ACCOUNTING RECORDS: DEFINITION, WHAT THEY INCLUDE, AND TYPES

Accounting records are all of the documentation and books involved in the preparation of financial statements or records relevant to audits and financial reviews. Accounting records include records of assets and liabilities, monetary transactions, ledgers, journals, and any supporting documents such as checks and invoices. Accounting records are all of the documents involved in preparing financial statements for a company.

Certain regulatory bodies require companies to keep their accounting records for several years in the event that they need to be reviewed.

Accounting records are often reviewed for audits, compliance checks, or other business related necessities.

Types of accounting records include transactions, general ledgers, trial balances, journals, and financial statements.

Understanding Accounting Records

Rules and laws are generally in place to force accounting entities and accounting firms to retain accounting records for a specified period of time. In the U.S., the Securities and Exchange Commission (SEC) requires that accounting firms retain records from audits and reviews for at least seven years and that they retain any records that support or cast doubt on the conclusions of an audit. There is no universal agreement as to which collection of business documents comprise a comprehensive set of accounting records. Accounting records can be thought of as a catch-all term. Different parties, such as creditors, equity investors, or groups interested in corporate governance will have different, and often competing priorities; their demands or preferences for documentation will continuously change.

At different points in the economic or business cycle, parties demanding accounting records will alter their request for information based on the position in a cycle. For instance, at the start of an upswing in a business cycle, requests for financial statements might be strong, as equity investors are bullish. In contrast, during a dip in a business cycle, creditors might require more details surrounding balance sheet items, as they become more hesitant to extend credit.In short, accounting records and even methods of accounting are continuously evolving to keep pace with the changing nature of business and the information demands of interested market participants.

Types of Accounting Records

Accounting records generally come in two forms: single entry and double entry. By its name, single entry is a much simpler method, which works better for smaller operations. The double entry method is more complex and requires two entries, one credit and one debit, for every transaction a business makes. The goal is to balance the books and account for the movement of cash through an organization. This is primarily done in larger corporations, which helps with spotting errors and potential fraud. The specific types of accounting records that are reviewed consist of the transactions, journals, general ledgers, trial balances, and financial statements of a company.

Transactions

The transaction is the starting point for any accounting
record. It is the catalyst for the entire process that shows
any item bought or sold, depreciated, etc., that a business
transacts.

Journals

Journals record all of the transactions that are made by a
company. Journals can cover all of the entire transactions
of a company or there can be different journals for different
areas of the firm. The only necessity is that journals are
kept up to date and that all the transactions are recorded in
some manner.

General Ledgers

The general ledger is the movement of transactions in the
journal to designated places in the general ledger that are
outlined by the type of transaction. This makes it easier to

comb through the transactions and categorize them correctly in the preparation of the trial balance and ultimately the financial statements.

Trial Balances

The trial balance is the summation of all credits and debits within the business cycle. Once this step has been completed, all entries should balance out. If they do not, this can reveal an error that must be corrected or possible fraud. It will be crucial to determine the disconnect.

Financial Statements

The financial statement is the final piece of document that comprises the components of all the other accounting documents. The financial statements are what will be provided to the public and to regulatory bodies for viewing. Investment analysts can review the financial statements to arrive at their thoughts on the company. Regulatory bodies can request the accounting documents that the financial statements were generated from to gain a deeper understanding of the company.

Competitive Intelligence: Definition, Types, and Uses

Competitive intelligence, sometimes referred to as corporate intelligence, refers to the ability to gather, analyze, and use information collected on competitors, customers, and other market factors that contribute to a business's competitive advantage. Competitive intelligence is important because it helps businesses understand their competitive environment and the opportunities and challenges it presents. Businesses analyze the information to create effective and efficient business practices.

HOW COMPETITIVE INTELLIGENCE WORKS

By definition, competitive intelligence assembles actionable information from diverse published and unpublished sources, collected efficiently and ethically. Ideally, a business successfully employs competitive intelligence by cultivating a detailed enough portrait of the marketplace so it may anticipate and respond to challenges and problems before they arise. Competitive intelligence transcends the simple cliché "know your enemy." Rather, it is a deep dive exercise, where businesses unearth the finer points of competitors' business plans, including the customers they serve and the marketplaces in which they operate. Competitive intelligence also analyzes how a wide variety of events disrupts rival businesses. It also reveals how distributors and other stakeholders may be impacted, and it telegraphs how new technologies can quickly render invalid every assumption.

Within any organization, competitive intelligence means different things to different people and departments. For example, to a sales representative, it may refer to tactical advice on how best to bid for a lucrative contract. To top management, it may mean cultivating unique marketing insights used to gain market share against a formidable competitor. The nature of competitive intelligence varies for different companies, depending on the industry, circumstance, and a host of other factors; for example, companies that are impacted by politics and laws might require information about statutory changes that could affect the company's operations. For any group, the goal of competitive intelligence is to help make better-informed decisions and enhance organizational performance by discovering risks and opportunities before they become readily apparent. In other words, competitive intelligence aims to prevent businesses from being caught off guard, by any oppositional forces.

Types of Competitive Intelligence

Competitive intelligence activities can be grouped into two main silos: tactical and strategic. Tactical intelligence is shorter-term and seeks to provide input into issues such as capturing market share or increasing revenues. Strategic intelligence focuses on longer-term issues, such as key risks and opportunities facing the enterprise. In either case, competitive intelligence differs from corporate or industrial espionage, which relies on illegal and unethical methods to gain an unfair competitive advantage.

Special Considerations

While most companies can find substantial information about their competitors online, competitive intelligence goes beyond grabbing such easily accessible, low-hanging fruit. Only a small portion of competitive intelligence involves trawling the Internet for information. A typical competitive intelligence study includes information and analysis from various disparate sources, including the news media, customer and competitor interviews, industry experts, trade shows and conferences, government records, and public filings. But these publicly accessible information sources are mere starting points. Competitive intelligence also encompasses investigating the full breadth of a company's stakeholders, key distributors, and suppliers, as well as customers and competitors.

For proof of the growing importance of competitive intelligence, look no further than the creation of the Society of Competitive Intelligence Professionals (SCIP), founded in the US in 1986. This global nonprofit group comprises a membership community of business experts across industry, academia, and government, who regularly congress build out intelligence infrastructure, share research decision-support tools, and advance collective analytical capabilities. This group, renamed "Strategic and Competitive Intelligence Professionals" in 2010, holds several national and international conferences and summits each year.

Top Ways to Manage Business Risks

Risk management has always been an important tool in running any business, particularly when a market experiences a downturn. In any economic environment, an unexpected surprise can destroy your business in one fell swoop if you didn't have the right risk management strategies in place to prevent, or at least mitigate, the damage from that risk. External risks are out of your control. These include, but are not limited to, interest rates, exchange rates, politics, and weather. Internal risks are in your control and include information breaches, noncompliance, lack of insurance, growing too fast, and many more. The following are some of the areas that business owners can focus on to help manage the risks that arise from running a business.

1. Prioritize

The first step in creating a risk management plan should always be to prioritize risks and threats. You can do so by using a somewhat universal scale based on each risk's likelihood of happening:

Very likely to occur

Some chance of occurrence

Small chance of occurrence

Very little chance of occurrence

Of course, a risk that falls into the top category should take priority over the others, and a plan to prevent, or at least mitigate, these risks should be put into place. However, there is a catch. If a risk falls into a lower rung yet presents the potential for more financial damage, then it should take priority.

2. Buy Insurance

Assess liabilities and legal regulations to determine what types of insurance will be required for your business. This might include:

Life insurance

Disability insurance

Professional insurance

Completed operations insurance

Buying insurance allows you to transfer your risk to insurance companies for a small cost, especially when compared to the potential cost of uncovered risk.

3. Limit Liability

If you're a sole proprietor, limit your liability by changing to a corporation or limited liability company (LLC). In this type of structure, the owner of the business is not held personally liable for the company's debts or other liabilities.

4. Implement a Quality Assurance Program

A good reputation is imperative if you want a sustainable business. Customer service is key to success. Be sure to test your products and services in order to assure the highest quality. By testing and analyzing what you're offering, you will have an opportunity to make necessary adjustments. Also, strongly consider taking it a step further by evaluating your testing and analyzing methods.

5. Limit High-Risk Customers

If you're just getting started, immediately implement a rule that customers with poor credit must pay ahead of time, which will avoid complications down the road. In order to do this, you must have a procedure to identify poor credit risks far in advance.

6. Control Growth

This has everything to do with employee training. If you're selling products and/or services and you set lofty goals for employees, they might be tempted to take unnecessary risks, which can lead to a bad reputation for your company. Instead, train your employees to focus on quality, not quantity. By doing so, you will avoid the risk of declining sales due to high-pressure sales tactics that customers don't appreciate. On a related note, while innovation is a key to success, you don't want to innovate too fast. If your company is constantly relying on the next innovation for growth, then a hiccup is inevitable because not all new products and services will be successful.

7. Appoint a Risk Management Team

If you want to save capital by not having to hire an outside firm, and there is time available, you can appoint current employees to head a risk management team. However, this would only be wise if someone within the team has experience in this area and can act as a leader. Otherwise, paying for an outside risk management team will be a worthwhile investment. They will be able to map out all the risks to your company based on your type of business and set up strategies to implement immediately if any of those risks become a reality. This should lead to the prevention, or mitigation, of those risks and threats.

Risk management is a form of insurance in itself and is an imperative step for sustainable success. The seven steps above should get you started in shaping a risk management plan, but they are just starting points. A deep dive into your business and industry will help you better shape a risk management plan that could save the business you worked hard to create.

STARTING A BUSINESS WITH NO MONEY: HOW TO BEGIN

Starting a business requires a certain amount of planning, which includes determining how much capital you'll need. It's possible to start a business with little or no money, but doing so can test the limits of your creativity and commitment. It's helpful to know what options you have if that's your goal and you intend to grow it on a shoestring.

Overcome the Challenges

An undeniable truth about starting a business is that money matters. A 2022 survey from Skynova, which aims to help small businesses get paid faster, asked startup founders to name their top reasons for failure. Forty-seven percent cited a lack of financing while 44% said that they simply ran out of cash. Starting a business with no money or minimal capital can limit what you can do to grow and scale in the early stages. For example, when you have no money it can be more difficult to:

Hire employees or support staff

Purchase necessary inventory or supplies

Advertise and market your business

How impactful a lack of money is can depend on the type of business you're hoping to start. If your budget is limited, then you might consider what kind of businesses you could start with zero investment.

Be sure to conduct market research before you even begin thinking about developing your idea. Determine who your competition is and how you plan to target your intended customer base. You may want to consider getting the opinions of potential customers through a focus group or via social media. You can also check with the Small Business Administration (SBA), which offers free educational resources to help you learn more about the basics of starting a business.

Develop a Low-Cost Business Idea

Some businesses cost more to start than others. For example, you may need $100,000 or more to open a restaurant while you may be able to get a food truck up and running for a fraction of that amount. The best businesses to start when you have no money are ones with minimal upfront costs. They're the kinds of businesses you might be able to start from home with nothing more than a laptop and an internet connection. Here are some of the best low-cost business ideas you might consider.

Content creation for online businesses

Freelance writing or blogging

Virtual assistant business

Social media manager or consultant

Online course creator or online tutor

Online bookkeeper

Dropshipping

eBay reseller

YouTube or TikTok creator

Graphic designer

Video editing

These are all businesses that you could run from home without having to spend a lot of money. There are also some businesses you can start offline that don't require startup cash. For example, you might start a dog-walking or pet-sitting business, become a tutor for local students, or teach art or music. These businesses allow you to leverage your skills to make money without spending any money. Be sure to check local laws first if you're interested in starting a business that's subject to regulation, such as a home daycare or home bakery.

The Critical Role of Budgeting

When starting any business, it's important to have a budget to follow. Your budget serves as a financial guide to help you understand your costs when getting your business off the ground. What your business budget looks like initially can depend on what kind of business you're starting. If you're pursuing a low-cost business plan, your startup costs may be much lower than someone who's starting a brick-and-mortar business. In terms of how to make a small business budget prior to launching, it's important to add up all of the costs you expect to have. That might include:

Purchasing inventory or supplies

Renting or leasing a business space

Buying equipment

Paying for marketing or advertising

Hiring staff

Your budget should be as detailed as possible so you have a realistic picture of what your spending might look like. You can then compare that to an estimate of what you expect your sales or revenue to be once your business launches. Budgeting for a business isn't something you do once, either. It's important to review your budget monthly to see how cash flows in and out of the business. Keeping expenses to a minimum is one of the best ways to maximize cash flow while your business is still in the fledgling phase.

Creative Financing Options

There are a number of ways to finance a new business without having to spend any money yourself. Comparing different options can help you decide what might be right for you. Consider the following options:

Small Business Grants: These grants provide money to support entrepreneurship, and unlike a loan, it doesn't need to be paid back. The SBA supports a number of grant programs, including ones for minority-owned, women-owned, and veteran-owned businesses.

Crowdfunding: This option allows people to contribute money to campaigns in small amounts in order to help entrepreneurs launch their businesses. Some of the most popular platforms for seeking support include GoFundMe, Indiegogo, and Kickstarter.

Microloans. If you're comfortable borrowing to fund your new business, you might consider a microloan. The SBA's microloan program allows you to borrow up to $50,000 to start a business and you can repay it over a period of up to six years.

Credit Cards: Business credit cards can help you to pay for the things you need to start or run your business and they can be easier to qualify for than loans. Depending on which business credit card you choose, you might be able to earn cash back, points, or travel miles on your purchases.

Peer-to-Peer (P2P) Lending: Peer-to-peer loans allow you to borrow money from the crowd. Investors contribute money to fund loans and borrowers pay them back over time, with interest. Loan rates and terms can depend on your overall creditworthiness.

Traditional small business loans might be harder to get if you're still in the beginning stages of starting a business. Lenders typically require you to have one to two years of operating history and a minimum level of revenue to qualify. Working on establishing business credit could help you to qualify for loans later once your business is up and running. If you're using a crowdfunding platform to raise money for a new business, be sure to read the fine print to understand what you'll pay in fees and what happens if your campaign isn't fully funded.

Bootstrapping Techniques

Bootstrapping simply means using the resources you have at hand to fund your business. Choosing to bootstrap a business could help you avoid taking on debt, but whether it's realistic can depend on your financial situation. BSome of the ways to bootstrap a business include:

Using funds in personal savings accounts or a certificate of deposit (CD)

Borrowing against your 401(k)

Taking an early withdrawal from an individual retirement account (IRA)

Pulling equity out of your home

Selling things you don't need for cash

Putting together a fundraiser locally to ask for donations

Asking friends and family for a loan

Each of these options has pros and cons. For instance, borrowing against your 401(k) or taking money from an IRA can shortchange your retirement savings since the funds you take out won't benefit from compounding interest. Not to mention, you could be subject to a 10% early withdrawal penalty on distributions. Taking a home equity loan or line of credit carries its own risks. If the business fails, you'll still be responsible for paying back what you've borrowed. Should you default on a home equity loan or line of credit, your home could end up in foreclosure. The bottom line is that before you bootstrap, it's important to look at both the advantages and disadvantages of doing so.

Leverage Free Resources

Starting a business is no easy task and you may need some help along the way. You could hire a business coach but that requires money, so it's helpful to know where you can find small business resources for free. Here are some of the places you can look to get free help when starting a business.

SBA: As mentioned, the SBA offers a number of resources to help small business owners, including the SBA loan program as well as educational articles covering how to start a business.

Small Business Development Centers: Small Business Development Centers are local organizations that assist small business owners with things like planning, accessing capital, and scaling for growth.

SCORE: SCORE is a network of mentors who help small business owners find success. Entrepreneurs can connect with a SCORE mentor to get help with planning and starting a business, growing a business, or exiting a business when they're ready to move on.

U.S. Department of Veteran Affairs: The VA offers support to veterans who are interested in starting small businesses. That includes access to educational resources and training for would-be business owners.

National Women's Business Council: The National Women's Business Council is committed to helping women entrepreneurs succeed. Specifically, that centers on helping women in STEM get the capital they need to start their businesses.

You can also check for free resources locally. For instance, your local chamber of commerce might sponsor free workshops or seminars aimed at helping budding entrepreneurs. You can also look for local nonprofits that serve the small business community.

If you're starting a business with no money, there's one more free resource you can utilize. Social media can be an effective way to market your new business without spending a dime on advertising. It may take a little longer to build an audience if you're not actively spending on ads, but it's a zero-cost way to spread the word about your business. The Federal Trade Commission (FTC) has specific rules for advertising and marketing that business owners must adhere to in order to avoid penalties.

Network and Collaborate

You might be starting a business on your own but if you want it to grow, it can be helpful to focus on building the right connections. That's where networking and collaborating come in. Having a sizable network could benefit you in different ways. For example, you might have a connection who could introduce you to someone who's interested in investing in your business. Or you might be offered an opportunity to promote your business on someone's podcast or YouTube channel, which is a great way to get free exposure.

In terms of how you build your network, it can depend on what type of business you have. If you're starting a brick-and-mortar business, for instance, then you might want to look for connections locally first. That might include joining your local chamber of commerce or small business development council. If you're starting an online business, then you could use online resources to connect. LinkedIn could be a good place to start your networking efforts. You can also branch out to other social media platforms to forge professional relationships with business owners or influencers in your niche.

Build a Robust Online Presence
With 62% of the world's population using the internet and 85% of Americans getting online every day, it makes sense to establish a virtual presence for your business. This can include setting up a website or blog, launching a YouTube

channel, getting active on TikTok, or building a presence on Facebook, X, or Instagram.

One of the best things about using social media to market a new business is that it doesn't have to cost anything. While you could spend money on ads, it's free to create profiles on social media platforms. If you're interested in setting up a website or blog for your business, platforms like Wix allow you to do that for free. If you want to build an online presence without spending money, you can certainly do so. It's also important, however, to think about which channels will offer the best return on investment for your time. Understanding where your potential customers gravitate when they're online can help you identify which social media channels are worth targeting.

What Is the Best Business to Start With No Money?

The best business to start with no money is the one that allows you to use your skills, knowledge, and resources in a way that produces maximum return and maximum enjoyment. If you love dogs, for example, then starting a dog-walking or pet-sitting business could be a good fit and it doesn't require a lot of money.

What Is the Easiest Business to Own?

The easiest business to own is one that generates passive income. Passive income is money that you earn without having to do a lot of ongoing work. For example, blogging can provide a passive income if you're making money from affiliate marketing or online ads. You could also make passive income by selling digital products that you only have to create once, such as printables, journals, or ebooks. It's possible to start a business with no money if you have an organized plan and strategy. Knowing what you'll need to do to get your business started is the first step. Once your business is up and running, you can explore the best ways to grow it in order to achieve the level of success you desire. That might include applying for small business loans, which can help you to scale and expand.

Ways to Impact the World With Your Business

It's common to think that starting a business is a means to making money. While you can start a business to make money, strive for more than that. If the sole reason for your business is to make money, you will be more apt to give up when your business isn't making money. Yet, if you tie a reason to why you're starting your business, now you're giving yourself a little extra push. There are thousands of entrepreneurs who have started a business to not only make money, but to make an impact on the world. I like to call the entrepreneurs who also make an impact on the world while earning an income, Philanthropreneurs.

1. Gain Clarity

There are a million and one businesses you can start. If you try to start too many businesses at once, you will wear yourself too thin. You'll want to pick one business that you know more than most and one that you feel can help make an impact on others. To help gain clarity, you need to have time to yourself. You'll want to take a day for yourself and write potential business ideas. From there, you'll want to research your ideas and see if there's a viable option to starting your business or if your idea is already in a saturated market. Remember, you want the business you start to withstand the test of time and not be involved with a fad or trend.

When you pick a business idea to work with, you'll want to make a commitment of six months to a year to allow yourself to make it through the hard times. At the end of the six months or a year, you'll want to set an exact day where you can analyze your business which will allow you to pivot or keep going in the direction you love.

2. Understand Your Purpose

Once you have the business you want, you must determine if the business is within the realm of your purpose. Is it something you feel comfortable with? Is it something that you can see yourself doing even when times get tough? If your business doesn't align with your purpose, you must take another day for yourself and research your other potential business ideas. Starting a business that aligns with your purpose and makes an impact isn't something that can be done overnight. It's a process that can take months, even years to complete.

3. Focus On Your Audience

Just because your business aligns with your purpose and you think it'll make an impact, you need to be sure that your potential customers would buy your product or service. Before investing your entire life's savings, you'll want to test if your audience will buy your product. You can create a website, but you don't want to blow thousands. You can run ads but don't spend hundreds. You'll know within six months if you've created a product your audience would want. You don't have to be perfect. Within six months doesn't mean you are making six-figures, but it means that you have had enough people who have purchased your product that you feel in your gut could become successful if you keep working on your business.

4. Align Your Impact With Your Income

If your first business fails, don't become discouraged. Marc said that he found too many potential entrepreneurs who give up too soon or fail without ever trying to start a business again. There are countless stories of entrepreneurs who failed, but didn't give up. Whatever business you end up being successful with, make sure that you always align your impact with your income. It's tempting to start a business that only makes money without aligning to your purpose, but as stated before, when the going gets tough, you will be more likely to give up.

5. Stay Focused On Your Mission

Not everything will work right when you start your business. It's expected that you will fail, but no matter how tough it gets, always stay focused on your mission and what you're trying to achieve. Because you started a business that aligns with your purpose and not just to make money, you understand that your business will push you to your limits. You will go further than you ever thought was possible and in return, you'll make more of an impact on the world and others than you thought imaginable.

6. Be Bold

No idea is too big. There's no reason you can't take a moonshot. Never let others tell you that your idea is stupid or impossible because it hasn't been done before. If you 100% believe in your heart that your idea will change the world, don't let others bring you down. Be BOLD in your life. The bigger you think, the bigger of an impact you have, and the more of an impact you have the greater your net worth will be. The biggest takeaway I got from Marc was never to think that you can't do something because if you believe in yourself and your idea enough, anything can be accomplished! It was a pleasure speaking with Marc and learning how you can impact the world by starting your business. Now, don't wait for tomorrow or the day after to gain clarity researching your potential business ideas because time moves fast and eventually one day you'll wish you had started that business, but there won't be any more time left and that, is not the life someone wanting to impact the world lives.

PURPOSE-DRIVEN ENTREPRENEURSHIP — HOW TO BUILD A BUSINESS THAT MAKES A POSITIVE IMPACT

1. Defining your purpose

Your business's purpose is the driving force behind your company's success. It is why you established your business and the driving force behind your brand. Every decision you make as a purpose-driven entrepreneur must align with your business's purpose. To determine your purpose, consider the difference you want to make in the world, addressing the societal and environmental issues you care about. Once you've established your purpose, integrate it into every aspect of your business, including your mission statement, branding and product or service offerings.

2. Creating a sustainable business model

A sustainable business model is essential in purpose-driven entrepreneurship, driven toward achieving long-term financial, societal and environmental sustainability. This allows for a balance between economic growth and social concerns while considering environmental impacts and ensuring that the business delivers value to its shareholders. Within this model, use renewable resources to reduce waste and carbon footprints. Opt for eco-friendly transportation options, such as electric cars or bicycles. Instead of conventional energy sources, be open to using green energy and energy-efficient systems. Be sure to use packaging materials that are recyclable or biodegradable.

At the same time, focus on providing fair wages and benefits to your employees and creating a positive working environment. This will encourage team productivity, cost-efficiency and better customer service, all of which contribute to the long-term success of your business.

3. Building a community

Building a community is fundamental in purpose-driven entrepreneurship as it enables the business to create a positive impact and a thriving brand. A community can consist of stakeholders, comprising customers, employees, suppliers and peers who share your values and beliefs. Creating a community allows for a sense of belonging and shared purpose where your customers can share their experiences with your brand, and you can reward them for their loyalty. You can create a platform for collaborative problem-solving where customers share insights on feedback regarding your product or services. Through this engagement with your community, you can more effectively understand their needs, making developments that align with your purpose and creating a greater impact in the world.

4. Measuring your impact

Measuring your impact is fundamental in building a purpose-driven business. Track your progress, identify areas that need improvement, and justify your impact to stakeholders. Establish clear sets of key performance indicators (KPIs) that align with your mission statement. Social or environmental audits can help identify areas for improvement, track progress over time and guide better corporate social responsibility policies. You can also use assessment tools, such as the B Impact Assessment, the B Corp certification or the Sustainable Development Goals (SDGs), to assess your company's impact on sustainability and set targets for improvement. Another way to measure your impact is by engaging with your community of stakeholders, including customers, employees and suppliers. Ask for feedback on your impact, and consider their suggestions for improvement or corrective action. You can also participate in industry forums and collaborate with other purpose-driven businesses to share insights and best practices.

5. Telling your story

Telling an authentic and meaningful story is vital in building a purpose-driven business. Storytelling enables you to connect with customers on an emotional and personal level, creating meaningful bonds that lead to brand loyalty. Your story should reflect your purpose and authenticity while being compelling. Utilize storytelling techniques like videos or images that appeal to human emotions. Share success stories, testimonials and the feedback you've received from customers or employees.

Leverage social media, blogs or other platforms to reach out to your customers and stay engaged with your community. Share what happens behind the scenes, and highlight efforts that contribute to making the world a better place.

6. Collaborate with other purpose-driven businesses

Collaboration is an essential aspect of purpose-driven entrepreneurship, allowing you to connect with other like-minded businesses to create a more significant impact. Use collaboration to seek new ideas, share key learnings and leverage best practices to achieve your business objectives. Collaborating is an excellent way of creating awareness of your brand while bringing diverse perspectives and skill sets to the table. Seek out like-minded organizations that share your purpose, and engage them in collaborations such as joint marketing campaigns, networking events and corporate social responsibility initiatives. Not only will it strengthen your brand's mission and purpose, but it will also create a lasting impact on society.

7. Stay agile and innovative

Purpose-driven entrepreneurship requires a mindset of agility and innovation. Entrepreneurs must be adaptable to the ever-changing business landscape, identifying new opportunities to innovate and trend with the latest developments. With that in mind, continuously review your business model and strategies while keeping abreast of the latest emerging trends and technologies. Stay curious and, where possible, experiment with innovative solutions or new technologies that better assist your business goals. Ask your employees and stakeholders to offer suggestions, and always be ready to pivot when necessary to deliver the best results for your business, customers and the wider society. Purpose-driven entrepreneurship presents a powerful way of building a successful and sustainable business while positively impacting society. By defining a clear purpose, creating an environmentally and financially sustainable business model, building a community, measuring your impact and telling your story, you can effectively differentiate your brand while creating a lasting legacy for future generations.

CONCLUSION

As a purpose-driven entrepreneur, your primary goal is to build a successful business and make a positive difference in the world. In today's world, consumers are becoming more mindful of their impact on the environment and society, leading to the increased demand for purpose-driven businesses.